NLP

The Greatest Beginner's Manual That Divulges Methods
For Mental Manipulation, Understanding People's
Thoughts, And Reading Minds To Your Benefit

*(The Complete Guide To Influencing Others Through The
Power Of Mind Control)*

Anto Martin

TABLE OF CONTENT

The Influence That Both The Conscious And Unconscious Mind Have On One Another 1

Hypnotic Rapport And Changing Perceptual Positions To Effect Behaviour Change 4

The Synopsis Of How NLP Can Completely Change Your Life 12

Powerspin: The Key To Developing Exceptional Learning States 19

A Look At The Shadow Side Of Manipulation .. 32

The Building Blocks Of The Shadow Side Of Nlp 46

How Does Neurolinguistic Programming (Nlp) Go About Changing People? 58

An Explanation Of Some NLP Techniques 63

Both NLP And Hypnosis Are Quite Useful. 77

Where Does It Fall Within The Umbrella Of Nlp? 83

What Kinds Of Effects Does Your Body Language Have On Your Mind? 89

Hypnosis 98

The Influence On Individuals 105

Deception 114

Methods To Gain Control Over Yourself, And Consequently, Your Life 125

NLP Techniques That Have Undergone Behavioral Alterations 139

Techniques From The Field Of Neuro-Linguistic Programming That May Be Used To Create Anchors 144

.... 144

Methods For Influencing The Mind 153

How Should One Go About Using The Anchoring Technique? 158

How Can You Overcome Your Tendency To Procrastinate With The Help Of NLP Techniques? 172

The Influence That Both The Conscious And Unconscious Mind Have On One Another

Have you ever given any attention to the possibility of altering one of your own personal habits? Just one of your bad habits will be broken. The pattern may consist of the following: • Is it feasible to give a presentation and remain calm throughout it, free of stress and anxiety?

• Decrease the total amount of time spent on social media, both in terms of minutes and hours.

• Do not put things off till later; instead, get them done as they should be done. • Decrease the amount of snacks you consume; for example, do not eat a whole bowl of ice cream or crackers in one sitting.

The Divided Mind of Consciousness and Unconsciousness

When that is accomplished, it will be feasible for you to realise your objectives. This is due to the fact that your subconscious mind believes that this is what you need at all times. When you agree to include the NLP, it is unquestionably similar to training your mind. The brain uses NLP as a manual most of the time, and when you accept to involve the NLP, it is certainly like training your mind. Training it to be fluent in the language of your thoughts, and once that has been accomplished, using it to assist you in solving problems. It acts as if it were a helping "server," and your unconscious mind will then be aware of what it is that you need and feel that it is essential to your existence.

NLP also requires excellent communication skills, both with the client and with other people. primarily conceived via the use of methods and designs that are lauded for their superiority and effectiveness. The majority of therapists that see positive outcomes with their patients make use of this technique. The majority of people have the misconception that NLP is only a collection of different strategies, methods, and tools. But in a more practical sense, it is much more than that; it is the mentality and the procedures that are used in order to know that the objectives that have been planned, as well as the approaches that are used in order to accomplish good outcomes. It is essential to have an understanding of the processes and procedures that are used in order to successfully cure and regulate your mind, as well as a person's emotional condition and, ultimately, their own life.

Hypnotic Rapport And Changing Perceptual Positions To Effect Behaviour Change

It is likely that you are familiar with the concept of rapport if you have spent any significant amount of time working in a field related to sales. You probably have some amount of understanding of what a report is. If you've taken any sales training classes or studied sales in college, then you probably already know that building rapport with potential customers is an important step in the sales process. When you initially meet a new prospective customer, one of the first things you should do is establish a rapport with that person (or people, depending on the circumstances), since this is one of the most important steps in the sales process.

In some of the sales training sessions I've been in, building rapport consisted of simply complementing a person on anything apparent in the room, such as a trophy, their dress, or something else in the room. But there is a definite separation between what most people have learned is rapport and what actually is hypnotic rapport, and that is what I want to talk with you today. There is absolutely nothing wrong with this, per se; nevertheless, there is a clear gap between what most people have learned is rapport and what precisely is hypnotic rapport.

I indicated to you in the first session that the most important aspect of communication is not what is said but how it is spoken, as well as how a message is conveyed via non-verbal interactions. The in-depth study of body language teaches students that it is common for the words that a person uses to express themselves to be utterly at odds with the meanings that their body language conveys. Therefore, I feel compelled to ask: should we accept individuals at face value in terms of what they say, ignoring all of the things that they are not expressing vocally but which their body is telling outwardly? Consider the implications. If someone's body language is telling you "No. I don't want to buy from you," but their words are saying "Yes. I want to buy from you," it's important to pay attention to both. I'm probably interested in it," is there a good chance that a sale will be made? Additionally, the opposite is also true. Whenever someone tells you "No. Should you trust them when they say, "I'm not interested," even when it is abundantly evident from their body language that they are, in fact, highly interested? That question seems to have answered itself. Nonverbal communication is something that everyone does, and it's something that happens naturally on an unconscious level. This may also be framed by referring to it as unconscious communication, which is another way of looking at it. When we have hypnotic rapport with another person, we are connecting with them on an unconscious level. In order to develop a connection via hypnosis, how precisely do we communicate subliminally? There are several methods, some of which will be covered in this lesson.

The first method I'm going to go through is called matching, and it comes from the field of NLP. When you successfully match what the other person is doing, both physically and through imitating their representational systems, you have successfully matched what they are doing. If the person in front of you is breathing at a quick pace, you will eventually learn to match their rate of breath. If a person is trying to communicate with you using their hands, you should mimic the same hand gestures that they are making. You should cross your right leg in response to someone else who has their right leg crossed. Your compatibility. You are mimicking the other person's nonverbal behaviour word for word, but you are doing it in such a way that it is not immediately apparent that you are making fun of their actions. This helps you create rapport with the other person.

I brought up the subject of representational systems. Stay tuned for the next chapter, in which we will cover these topics; in the meanwhile, I ask for your patience and cooperation.

Mismatching is the next strategy that I'd like to discuss with you. It is possible that there may be times over the course of the sales call in which it will be essential for you to disconnect from the prospective client. For instance, when it is time to move on to the next potential customer. When you mismatch someone, you start acting in a way that is counter to how you would normally match them. You start acting in a way that is purposefully different from what they are doing. In the field of neuro-linguistic programming (NLP), this phenomenon is referred to as a pattern interrupt for the same reason that it disrupts the relationship and the flow of communication and connection.

Pacing and leading is the last strategy that I am going to discuss for the time being. Another one of NLP's techniques, this one refocuses on an individual's internal emotional state rather than on the person's physiology or representational systems in order to establish rapport with them. There are specific physiological indications that we identify with excitement that occur when someone is enthusiastic, such as increased heart rate and sweating. We can hear enthusiasm in the individual's voice, and we can also see excitement in the individual's facial expressions and other body motions as they grow more lively. The first step in pacing is identifying an individual's current emotional state and then adapting the pace to fit that mood. After you have timed their emotional or mental condition, the next step is leading, which is really when you start to make subtle shifts in your own emotional state, which in turn induces them to make shifts in their own emotional state. If a prospective client is not in a condition of readiness to make a purchase when you walk in to introduce yourself to them, you may match whatever state they are in at that specific time to create rapport with them, and then you can begin to guide their emotional state in another way, which is a state of readiness to make a purchase. By the way, excitement is a condition that encourages purchasing. When a prospective consumer feels enthusiastic about your offer, it puts them in a state of mind that is optimal for making a purchase of your product or service. Keep in mind that individuals make purchases based on their emotions and then try to explain those decisions with reasoning after the fact. If a person is not in the appropriate frame of mind, they will almost certainly reject anything you propose to them, and even if they do buy something, you can be sure that they will not be satisfied with it. Building rapport is thus of utmost significance in the process of making sales.

The Synopsis Of How NLP Can Completely Change Your Life

Will the use of NLP bring about any changes in your life? After completing the NLP classes, it became very evident to me that I would never be satisfied with anything, particularly if it meant continuing to work at a job that I despised. The passion I had and the goals I wanted to accomplish were the deciding factors for me. After leaving my work, I haven't even bothered to look back, and the primary reason for that is the encouragement and support I received from my wife. I used to be dissatisfied with my job, but things have changed for the better, and now I make much more money while putting in less hours.

I am also able to go into large gatherings of people without feeling timid or frightened, and I have began to confront my anxieties while simultaneously being able to discover the inner and outer serenity that I have been seeking for a very long time as a result of this. These are both positive aspects of my experience. This was just an extremely brief email to let everyone know that miracles have been taking place, and I am grateful to you for making it possible.

Where Do You Stand in Your Life?

The aforementioned quotation is only one of the countless testimonies that demonstrate how NLP has significantly improved the quality of someone's life. Every day, I receive emails like this one, and they make my heart feel like it's about to explode with enthusiasm. However, after reading such letters, I also discover news about all of the anti-NLPers that exist in the globe.

'

It is not a secret that neuro-linguistic programming, sometimes known as NLP, has emerged as a topic that is fraught with controversy. NLP is valuable in many fields, including business, education, coaching, and personal development; nonetheless, many people continue to dismiss it as something that is overvalued and pointless, despite the fact that its benefits cannot be contested. These complaints are almost often voiced by those who have no prior experience with NLP of any kind. Due to the fact that Neuro-linguistic Programming is still the subject of a significant amount of study and controversy as a result of the fact that it is a science that has not yet been completely uncovered, it gets a lot of negative criticism. The main issue that has to be asked is whether or not NLP is worth the investment, and whether or not it will really make a difference in your life.

Before you go any farther into this subject, though, I feel obligated to warn you of something.

There is in fact no truth, just how one chooses to interpret the world.

Even before I begin each of my workouts, I will often repeat these phrases to myself. Those who are interested in supporting the trainings offered by NLP will learn that in addition to the tools that are used, NLP also teaches the manner, or the attitude, that will allow an individual to effect change and witness outcomes.

• Natural Language Processing teaches its students to have a curious mindset. • One of the tenets of NLP is to have an open mind. • The NLP curriculum includes classes on adaptability.

It is possible that the concept of NLP is difficult to understand since there are not actually any facts that can be seen; nonetheless, there are models. It is ultimately up to the individual to decide whether or not they will embrace these models.

The applied teachings from NLP will provide the finest outcomes for those who are mature enough and open-minded enough to indulge their natural inquisitiveness.

It is true that "the mind, just like a parachute, only works when it is opened." Professor Krasner

It is not so much a question of whether or not one should have doubts about NLP as it is about making NLP work and putting in the necessary effort to make it work.

The students who take the NLP course will learn how to put into practise the method of thinking that works best for them. They will come to understand how the new information will result in a shift in their belief in themselves. In addition to this, the significance of one's life, spirituality, profession, relationships, physical fitness, and overall health will be emphasised. It is all about teaching them how to modify their way of thinking automatically into something that they can better adapt to their own particular routines and transform those unhelpful reactions into something useful.

Negative ideas, feelings, and restrictions will be eradicated, and so will fear and hurdles, with which they will be provided guidance on how to cope.

Along with being satisfied with who they are and how they feel about themselves, as well as making goals for the future and achieving those objectives, self-acceptance and forgiving of others will be taught as part of this course. It's almost as if they're doing miracles in their own lives.

Even though there is currently very little data that demonstrates the efficacy of NLP from a scientific standpoint, there are still a great deal of testimonials that demonstrate that it is effective. When scientists have figured out a means to evaluate success, fulfilment, and happiness, that day will finally arrive.

NLP, or neuro-linguistic programming, is really simply about regulating and training your mind, which is actually quite a crucial ability to have in life, particularly when it comes to being happy and successful in life.

Is it possible that learning NLP may really transform a person's life? Whether or if that particular individual wants to participate is entirely up to them.

Powerspin: The Key To Developing Exceptional Learning States

We are able to practically permanently attach one emotional state to another by making proper use of the brain's programming instructions. This is analogous to how you would attach veneers of wood to form plywood.

Any one condition will immediately activate the others, and the combined effect will be very potent. Some people refer to this as "layering," and although each state continues to exist independently, they all operate together in an almost instantaneous manner.

Additionally, it is conceivable to combine several emotional states in order to produce what is essentially an entirely new state of mind.

You are able to create a totally new and potent learning programming code by using the Powerspin approach, which gives you the flexibility to select and choose among a variety of learning stages. In a later section, we are going to discuss the layering method. When you add new data or programming to your brain, you have completed a stage of the learning process known as neuroplasticity.

Step 1: Identify a circumstance in which you might benefit from having access to a diverse array of learning methods while you are in the process of acquiring new information.

2. For each of the following learning processes, go back to a period when you were effectively using that specific learning style or pattern.

A point in time when you realised that you now had access to information (programmes or data) that you did not have before beginning that learning process.

Engage your senses fully in the process of learning in this manner, and assign a distinct hue to each emotion you experience.

(a) Learning through inference or deduction

This may be seen as REASONING on our part. Trying to find a solution to a quadratic equation: oh, who created those enormous horrifying pictures then? To put it another way, I want to purchase anything from you. You informed me that it is 77 pence. You do the maths and determine that I should get 23 cents in return for my offer of one pound.

Another illustration: if we have found that ALL tall and slender persons grew up too quickly and we know that Joe is tall and slim, we may assume that Joe must have grown up too quickly since he is tall and skinny. Deduction was a strong skill for Sherlock Holmes.

Find an example from your own life that illustrates the way you like to study, and describe the colour of that feeling.

(b) Learning by induction

This kind of learning is also referred to as inferential learning. Making broad generalisations based on a single or several encounters while being ignorant of all relevant information.

Someone fired their gun. Blood was found on Fred's clothing when he was found nearby the crime site. It is possible that Fred is the one who committed the murder. But now we know that Fred is a veterinarian who was just nearby providing first aid to a hurt animal, therefore our assumption was absolutely incorrect.

When someone spends a lot of time discussing a certain topic, it leads us to believe that they have done significant research on that topic. When we verify our assumptions with them, we discover that we were right all along.

Find an instance in your own life when you successfully learned something using that method, and assign a colour to the sensation of learning something new.

(c) Memorization by rote

We may call this kind of learning REPETITION-BASED LEARNING. We acquire knowledge by having it explained to us or being demonstrated to us that "this is the way it is" or "this is the way to do it." When this action is carried out repeatedly, the information eventually gets ingrained in our minds as a fact, principle, technique, or belief. Learning the correct spelling of a term is referred to as ROTE. Which one should it be? Favour or favour? It is dependent on your location.

The majority of mathematical equations were inferred when they were first developed, but we now learn them via ROTE as a technique to tackle specific problems.

Learning by repetition has a tendency to discourage innovative thought.

Find an example from your own life that illustrates the way you like to study, and describe the colour of that feeling.

b) Imitating or serving as a model

It's possible that some people call this "copying" others' work. We acquire the ability to communicate verbally by first being attentive to others and then making an effort to imitate their behaviours. We keep a close eye on and ear out for feedback from our surroundings in order to determine whether or not we are correctly replicating the actions of people who have achieved success.

When I was a kid, I would watch my dad use a handsaw to cut things. A child's carpentry kit was provided to me, and I occupied myself with attempting to saw through the leg of the dining table. My ability to imitate my father's behaviour was pretty good, and as a result, I was successful but also disliked with my newly gained talent.

Find an example from your own life that illustrates the way you like to study, and describe the colour of that feeling.

(e) Learning via creative means

One way to approach learning like this is via the lens of NEW IDEAS. This is where comedic and artistic expression, as well as the so-called quantum jumps, come from. It's possible that we're coming up with fresh colour schemes for a bedroom and "discovering" how they appear. In the event that it is novel and distinct, our creative ability will have contributed to our encounter with new information, a unique kind of learning.

Find an example from your own life that illustrates the way you like to study, and describe the colour of that feeling.

(f) Testing or learning via experimentation

A young kid who is playing with bricks is investigating their surroundings and learning about gravity or anything else.

Through testing, it was determined that the square blocks would not fit into the circular holes.

There is a possibility that we may try a new cake mix or a different method for preparing veggies.

Find an example from your own life that illustrates the way you like to study, and describe the colour of that feeling.

At this point, you should have SIX different hues, one for each learning method.

You may have realised that in some learning settings, you are already combining or perhaps stacking several learning methods. This is probably something that you are doing unconsciously.

3. Visualise a circle that has been cut into six equal parts, and place the colour associated with one learning method in the first part of the circle, the second colour in the second part of the circle, and so on, until each of the six parts has a different hue.

4. Now, picture yourself gazing through a tube that is constructed in such a manner that as you go down the length of the tube, you are only able to view one section at a time.

Therefore, at first, the only colour that appears in your thoughts is colour number one. You will need to rotate the disc or circle until you can make out half of the number one and half of the number two. Keep turning the disc until you can see no other colour but the second one. You need to continue turning the disc until you have experienced all of the different hues.

Now give the disc a faster and faster spin until the colour you see is a jumble of all six hues, much like the jumbled appearance of colour that results when a youngster spins a top.

Give the hue a name, such "pinky blue," for example.

5. Peer through the rosy-blue haze and take another look at the picture from step 1 (the circumstance in which you wish to learn).

It's almost like looking at the world through rose-colored glasses, only in this case you get to choose the colour and create the glasses yourself.

This procedure was developed by collaboration with a dance instructor. He need a method of inducing specific mental and emotional states in order to fulfil his requirements. In the past, I have utilised procedures in which I have asked clients to assign a colour to their sensations. In addition to that, I recalled seeing a stage that was illuminated by a light that had a rotating disc of various colours. The tint of the whole stage shifted as the light passed through each of the different colours. Something quite similar has also been seen by me on a dance floor.

This worked out well for him, and he was able to assign a colour to each distinct feeling, as well as combine and mix those emotions to suit his needs.

It is essential to obtain the FEELINGS or EMOTIONS associated with the learning method, and it is also essential to give the FEELING a colour.

A Look At The Shadow Side Of Manipulation

We are aware that manipulators are present in our world and that they are all around us, but who precisely are these people? Who are these people and what kind of personality do they have? They are the spouse in a romantic relationship who is violent and controlling, causing damage not just to the connection the two of you have formed but also bringing your self-esteem down along with it. When it comes to the dynamics of a family, this individual is the member of the family that perpetually sows discord and disorder or the person who craves to be the focus of everyone's attention at all times. It might be a sibling, a parent, an aunt, an uncle, a cousin, or even a mother or father that makes cryptic comments with the intention of making others around them feel inferior or uncomfortable.

It's possible that the manipulator is your next-door neighbour or a friend of yours who likes to spread rumours and gossip. This individual takes pleasure in setting two people against one other and then stepping aside to watch them fight. At work, the manipulator may be a coworker who has a history of being dishonest and unethical, who is prepared to descend as low as they can to achieve what they want and who steps on the toes of everyone else on their journey to the top of the company. Out on the streets, the manipulators are the crooks and con artists who depend on deceit and diversion to scam you out of your hard-earned cash. These con artists will rob you in broad daylight without you being aware of it, and then they will silently conceal their traces to avoid being discovered.

The manipulator may come in any shape or form, sometimes in the type of person you least expect, and among the various things that a lot of these manipulators have in common is the fact that they suffer from some sort of personality disorder that makes them who they are. The manipulator can come in any shape or form, sometimes in the kind of person you least expect. In the year 1835, a physician by the name of Dr. James Cowles Prichard came up with the term "moral insanity" to describe a group of people who, although they were not technically insane according to the standards of today, exhibited very significant and distinguishing differences in their attitudes and the way they behaved with regard to matters of morality, ethics, and their emotional reactions or responses to particular situations. Prichard used the term "moral insanity" to describe these individuals. Despite these apparent distinctions when compared to other persons, those who were categorised as having moral insanity expressed very little social or emotional discomfort about their behaviour. This is because moral insanity is a kind of moral depravity.

These people had a lengthy history of emotional, psychological, relational, and behavioural challenges that were very considerably different from that of their family or even their society. These persons had a personality disorder of some form. Their dysfunctional behaviour patterns intruded into almost every facet of their lives, which led to difficulties in their capacity to function emotionally and personally. This, in turn, is likely one of the contributing factors to their manipulative tendencies. Some examples of the kinds of personalities that are more likely to turn to manipulative tactics are as follows:

The individual with this pervasive behaviour has a tendency to seek attention and resort to exaggerated displays of emotion, which is commonly referred to as being dramatic. This person has a personality type known as the histrionic personality type. They are capable of engaging in extremely manipulative behaviour when they are in a romantic relationship in order to acquire what they want.

The antisocial personality types are persons that have little respect for the underlying social standards that the majority of people in society adhere to. As a result, these people are capable of becoming manipulative. These antisocial personalities could consist of a variety of behaviour patterns, such as being unsupportive, chronically unreliable and irresponsible, conning others, and for those who have no regard for the fundamental rights of others, they could even resort to criminal activity and show no remorse for it. These behaviours are all examples of antisocial personality traits. According to clinical standards, these persons are very self-centered, and among the various behavioural patterns they can possibly display, some of those patterns include lying, fraud, intimidation, and even physical attack.

The Borderline Personality Disorder is characterised by persons who, when it comes to their self-perception, their emotions, and their relationships, may be passionate, volatile, and unstable. They have little to no ability to control their impulses, and the common characteristics associated with this type of behaviour include a fear of being abandoned, instability when it comes to their self-image and social relationships, displaying inappropriate but intense feelings of anger and paranoia, and even resorting to impulsive or self-damaging acts such as abusing substances or alcohol. Because of this instability, they are more likely to engage in behaviours that include manipulation.

Having a narcissistic personality is a disease that may lead to a feeling of entitlement, a desire to be praised, and an exaggerated sense of one's own self-worth. Narcissists also tend to have an inflated perception of their own self-worth. It is very rare for people with these characteristics to have a large ego, and they tend to care little about anybody other than themselves. This lack of empathy for others, arrogance, inflated self-esteem, and sense of entitlement, which leads them to think that they deserve to have special advantages and attention, may lead to emotions of jealously or envy when their needs are not being satisfied. This lack of empathy for others can also lead to a sense of entitlement, which leads them to believe that they deserve to have special privileges and attention.

This great feeling of entitlement causes them to believe that they have the right to punish or seek vengeance on anybody whom they perceive as failing to give them the attention, fair respect, or admiration that they think they deserve. As a result, they believe that they have the right to punish or exact revenge on anyone. Narcissism is not capable of true self-love from a psychological standpoint. This is due to the fact that individuals who battle with narcissism are more in love with the comical and idealised, unrealistic picture of themselves that they have made up in their thoughts.

The fact that these people have delusions of grandeur inside them is what causes them to behave in such a dysfunctional manner, and it's also the primary reason why others characterise them as being demanding, self-centered, condescending, and manipulative the vast majority of the time. Their friendships, family life, sexual connections, and even professional relationships are not safe from their narcissistic tendencies, and what makes it even more difficult is that persons with this personality disorder are resistant to change, preferring, instead, to demand others to adhere to their requirements. This makes it much more difficult for those who have to deal with them.

Behaviour that is Adaptable to Change

Being adaptable in one's behaviour is the last component of the NLP foundational model. This is the realisation that sometimes what you are doing is not truly working for you, and the subsequent realisation that it is vital for you to adjust those actions in order to ensure that you can figure out a way to make things work. This is the realisation that sometimes what you are doing is not actually working for you. You will have the ability to realise that there are times when it is time to let go of what you have tried in favour of new approaches that may really work for you better. You will be able to do this after you have gained this awareness.

When you acquire this kind of flexibility, you are accomplishing two different goals at the same time. To begin, by doing this, you are assuring that you can locate a method that is effective in assisting you in achieving your objective. You should make it a priority to guarantee that, at the end of the day, you are able to accomplish those objectives that you have set for yourself. Nevertheless, it is not all that takes on in this particular circumstance. In addition to this, you will be boosting resiliency. You acknowledge that things did not go according to plan, and as a result, you are able to demonstrate flexibility towards the situation.

Keep in mind that the focus of NLP is on the positive. It is important that you keep in mind that while you cannot always control the results of an event, you can influence how you react to it. That is precisely what it means to be flexible in your behaviour; it is acknowledging that you have tried something that did not work, and as a result, they are able to see exactly how they need to adjust in order to have the greatest possible opportunity of success.

By using this engaging image, authors Romilla Ready and Kate Burton explain how the four pillars may be applied to your day-to-day life and how they can help you achieve your goals.

Imagine that you decided to purchase a new piece of software that would assist you in keeping track of the names, addresses, phone numbers, and any other pertinent information about your friends and customers. You invest time and money into obtaining and installing the programme, only to find that it does not function properly because it has a code error.

You call the customer support department of the software firm, but the representatives there are impolite and unable to assist you. You have reached a stage when you need to use your talents at creating rapport with the customer service manager so that they would listen to your problems. It is necessary for you to improve your sensory awareness by paying close attention to what is being spoken to you, taking charge of your emotions, and selecting the action that is most appropriate in the given situation. In order to have productive conversations with the customer service manager, you need to have a clear idea of the result you want to achieve; do you want a replacement or a refund? Last but not least, you need to be ready to adjust your behaviour to accommodate a variety of outcomes in the event that the intended one cannot be attained.

You will become a better communicator and be able to attain the things you desire without a lot of stress or aggravation if you learn how to use NLP effectively, which is how it works.

The Building Blocks Of The Shadow Side Of Nlp

The Roots of the Shadow Side of NLP

In order to have a theoretical understanding of what Dark NLP is, one must first have a conceptual understanding of the ideas that form the foundation of NLP. NLP had its start when two persons named Bandler and Grinder encouraged a group of ideas about human behaviour and what it very well may be designed for. These ideas eventually became known as neuro-etymological programming, which is more often known as NLP. Initially, the techniques were quite mysterious; but, throughout that time period, they became much more accessible as a result of the work of brilliant individuals such as Tony Robbins and Derren Brown. Despite the fact that more people are aware of NLP than at any other point in recent history, relatively few people have the skills to effectively use it.

The showcasing of human behaviour in conjunction with phonetic norms obtained from academics like Noam Chomsky led to the development of the key concepts that underpin NLP. These two primary influences are combined into a set of formal criteria that investigate people's inspirations and the ways in which those influences might be shown and manifested. Formalising the concepts and principles that drive human behaviour has been summed up by one of the organisers of NLP as the area of emphasis that the organisation focuses on.

Subjectivity, awareness, and learning are the three basic areas that NLP uses to divide its concepts into distinct categories. According to the teachings of

NLP, there is no straightforward or objective comprehension of the world around us. Instead, each person constructs their own image of the world, which is comprised of the information received through the five senses as well as the language the individual learns to connect to their tangible information. It is hypothesised that the combination of concrete evidence and figurative language leads to behaviours that, in the long term, are either effective in accordance with our emotional map of the world or maladaptive and hazardous to our own aims and objectives.

When it comes to how it could perceive the human psyche as having both an aware and an oblivious side, NLP is typically in agreement with traditional brain research. This is one area in which NLP is generally in agreement. NLP education is built, in large part, on the belief that a significant amount of influence is exerted at the level of human thought that is associated with one's inner thoughts. People are defenceless against being manipulated in ways that they are unable to comprehend being controlled.

NLP views people as behaving in ways that are indicated by three essential perspectives: 'what the future contained', 'why'. The 'what the future held' behaviour and physiology that an individual demonstrates in a given circumstance, the 'how' manages the internal speculation designs that the individual has that administer their example of navigation, and the 'why' manages the supporting convictions, suspicions, and values that point an individual in one direction rather than another.

If you are able to grasp the three perspectives that were discussed before, then you will be able to demonstrate the whole of the truth about another person's actions. Rather than merely approximately mimicking the outside behaviour on its own, the emphasis should be placed on the fact that the internal cycle is being repeated, which is what causes the external conduct. Without the getting on with the inner components, the behaviour will most likely look to be dishonest and fake.

NLP encourages moving beyond the practise of passively accepting the many factors that might affect an individual's behaviour. Assuming that everything stays the same, it promotes doing thorough research and exercising effective control over the relevant components in order to determine the connections that exist among them and identify those that are essential to achieving the desired result. The traditional perspective and the NLP model of acquiring practises are somewhat different from one another in a number of significant ways. People have been known to acquire new behaviours the old-fashioned way, which involves accumulating their knowledge one piece at a time until they have enough to form the new behaviour as a complete. In the context of neuro-linguistic programming (NLP), "doing things backwards" means providing a person with all of the components of a behaviour immediately after it has been introduced, and then gradually removing those components one by one until the individual is only confronted with the core characteristics of the behaviour.

How to Make the Most of Your NLP for Success

Everyone harbours the desire to achieve greatness. The drive to take action in order to accomplish one's objectives is the defining characteristic of genuinely outstanding individuals as opposed to just average people. People that aspire to greatness do not put things off or tell themselves, "Someday, I'll be everything that I want to be." Instead, they begin taking significant action right away.

Taking action might be challenging for some people. It's possible that the conditions make you feel constrained. You can also be suffering from a lack of drive. However, they are only mental roadblocks that need to be overcome. You are able to overcome these roadblocks and go on with your plans. Your dreams of becoming greatness may become a reality.

Always keep in mind the definition of excellence. It's having the drive and the guts to push back against your own self-doubt. It is the energy required to take on challenges, no matter how great or minor. It is the aspiration to perform at a level higher than you are now capable of. Magnificence radiates.

If you want to be great, you should model yourself after those individuals who are great and successful. These individuals embody the best qualities of both dreamers and doers. They take the things that they dream about and strive hard to make them come true. They wake up quite early and stay up much beyond their bedtime. They do not allow worry or any other kind of mental impediment to stop them from accomplishing what is necessary and what they desire to do. They most often engage in healthy behaviours on a regular basis, which enables them to deal well with stress. You should make an effort to adopt their way of life so that the space in your life for achieving greatness is created in your routine. Additionally, you need to work on being more organised. Organisation enables you to devote certain amounts of time to the accomplishment of your objectives and to do it in a methodical manner.

If you also utilise NLP to begin overcoming the obstacles that may psychologically impede you from attaining your goals and aspirations, you will find that despite the fact that these activities may seem to be difficult, they are really pretty simple. In most cases, if you believe "I can't" or "That is impossible," you are incorrect in your assessment of the situation. You are unable to take action because you are experiencing some kind of mental barrier. The only way to achieve success is to push through those barriers and make the most of the inherent qualities you were born with.

How Does Neurolinguistic Programming (Nlp) Go About Changing People?

Practitioners of NLP often assert, among other things, that the field is equipped with a variety of techniques that may assist individuals in undergoing transformation.

This encompasses conditions such as a lack of self-assurance, hesitancy over making choices, worry, and anxiety.

Therefore, what is the fundamental strategy?

Only information is provided in this chapter. It should not be construed as reflecting any type of training for therapeutic treatments, nor should any of the other passages in this ebook either.

NLP practitioners, on the other hand, assert that they are able to assist us with issues such as insufficient self-assurance, ambiguity about choices, tension, and worry.

Some additionally claim that their product may be used therapeutically to treat severe diseases such as anxiety, phobias, addiction, and post-traumatic stress disorder (PTSD). However, due to the paucity of research that has been peer-reviewed and the absence of appropriate monitoring, I would dismiss these claims and advise anybody in need of assistance to seek it from properly competent medical, psychiatric, or psychological practitioners. Your health is too crucial to entrust to the care of well-meaning but inexperienced individuals.

Having said that, the fundamental premise that NLP adheres to for effecting change is astonishingly straightforward.

The practitioner is responsible for first gaining an understanding of the current condition of their client, sometimes known as the client's existing "map of their world," and then guiding the client to the desired, more resourceful state (a new map of their world).

They will do this in the following six steps:

1. The Result That Is Wanted

To begin, the practitioner will try to get an understanding of the change that the client wishes to accomplish in their life. They will assist the customer in setting "well-formed outcome" goals, which are assertions of the intended state that serve as a solid foundation upon which to build.

2. Model of the World To understand their client's present model of the world, use strategies such as creating rapport, obtaining a personal history, using the Meta Model and Meta Programs, and values elicitation. 3. Loosen the Model

You may weaken the unfavorable parts of the client's vision of the world by making use of tools such as the Logical Levels vision and the Milton Model.

4. Work in Changing

These are the key therapeutic strategies that are responsible for bringing about the transformation. Techniques such as anchoring, reframing, submodality shift, parts integration, visual squash, and time line treatment are all examples of tools that may be used.

5. Do the Cleaning

At this level, the focus is on integrating the changes the client has undergone into their overall way of being in a manner that is entirely compatible with their new selves. In addition to this, it is a practical method of identifying any little modifications that have not taken place yet but may be implemented throughout the session.

6. The Pace of the Future

The last step is when the practitioner assists the client in seeing themselves in their new condition and in projecting that state forward into the sorts of circumstances in which they would have either shown undesirable behaviors or attitudes or not felt as if they had the tools to cope. In this stage, the practitioner is helping the client to envision themselves in their new state. The goal here is to instill confidence in them by demonstrating that the improvements are in fact taking place.

An Explanation Of Some NLP Techniques

Please accept my greetings and have a blessed day! Thank you for joining us for this really stunning session. I really hope that the last meeting was informative and helpful to you. During this session, we will discuss the relevance of NLP as well as processes that are capable of bringing about outstanding outcomes. There will be a question regarding how the results of using NLP approaches were obtained. The answer to that question is something in the range of 85-90%; it has been confirmed, which is astonishing from a scientific standpoint.

People have found success in implementing NLP concepts using the following three methods:

The individual's level of understanding and application of the NLP procedures is the single most important factor in determining that person's level of success with those approaches.

-

The efficacy of the trainer is important, as is the manner in which he or she instructs you (often via the use of repetition of methods to ensure that you remember them). Students of NLP will benefit from having access to a skilled teacher who has the appropriate mindset since this will enable them to correctly implement the methods and make them more useful in their everyday life. Taking this course gives those who already possess these practical abilities the opportunity to further their careers and reach new milestones of achievement.

Simply said, if you include these NLP strategies into your day-to-day activities, you will experience an increase in your level of energy beginning when you get up and continuing until you go to sleep. The benefit of using NLP methods is that you will not have the experience of having a lower energy level or of feeling less inspired to do your task. You will not feel this way at all.

What aspects of our performance may be enhanced by using these NLP techniques? Everyone wants to live a life of greatness, as I have said in earlier songs and recordings that I have made. They want tranquility as well as an abundance of financial opportunities. They are looking for ways to boost their motivation and energy levels, as well as the capacity to find solutions to their medical or financial issues. To simplify things overall, it is essential that all of these tasks be completed as soon as possible. The skills of NLP are useful in this field, particularly when it comes to establishing connections. There are certain individuals who find it more challenging to meet with a client and sell a product; hence, we will discuss several strategies in subsequent modules in order to assist with activities linked to sales. This will assist you in reaching your goals in the professional world.

Last but not least, some individuals struggle with worries, phobias, or negative thinking. They will start to experience results if they comply with the guidelines of NLP and if they do the exercises in the manner that the trainer has instructed them to do.

The Presuppositions Behind the Very First Rule of NLP The meaning of response

When you communicate with another individual, it is expected that you would explain the significance of what you are saying to them in their own words. In point of fact, this is not the case. When you communicate, you bring with you some knowledge that has significance for you on the inside, but you want the other person to grasp it in the same way that you do. As a result, your conduct, such as the way you speak, do things, and move about, etc., will mirror your message and assist you convey what it is that you want to communicate while also ensuring that you get an acceptable reaction.

When it comes to communication, it is not always the case that other people will react to what you are saying in the manner that you intend if you speak properly and others hear what you are saying. You have to come to terms with the fact that the duty you have in terms of good communication does not cease after you have conveyed what you have to say.

You have to come to the realization that what you say is what the other person hears, but what it means to you on the inside is slightly different from what it means to them. This is something that you need to be aware of. As a result, you need to acknowledge the possibility that they may reply in a manner that is distinct from what you anticipate, and behave accordingly in order to ensure successful communication. This indicates that it is really important to pay great attention to the reaction that you get. What is brilliant and sparkling to you could strike someone else as unsatisfying or highly upsetting in their view. This can be true even if the same thing is presented in a different way. If they do not reply in the manner that you had hoped, you may need to adjust the method that you interact with them until you have the response that you want or something that is roughly equivalent to what you require. There can be situations when you discover that the answer you get is much superior to what you had anticipated! That is what it is to have awareness. It involves coming to terms with the fact that it is quite feasible to do even more than you had hoped.

When we communicate with one another, we often misinterpret one another for a variety of different reasons. One is that people's life experiences, as reflected in the words they use in their language, are uniquely individual to each person. For instance, when you say "Chinese," you could immediately think, "yummy," whereas someone else might react with distaste at the first mention of the word. As you can see, this is one word, yet the answers to it are radically different from one another while sharing the same meaning.

Maps and territories are subject to the second rule.

It's possible that the majority of the time, you don't function based on what is actual, but that you tend to rely on your map of what is real. If you want to be a good communicator, you need to know that what you represent to arrange what you have encountered in the world is not truly the world, i.e. the territory. This is necessary in order to be able to communicate effectively. You have to make a distinction between the numerous layers that make up your map and the maps of other people. First and first, there is the actual world, and your experiences in the world come in second place. What one individual has experienced of the world is not always indicative of what another has had the opportunity to encounter. You are the only one who can develop a model of what your universe is, and this model, in addition to being one of a kind and distinct from all the others, is also continuously evolving as more time passes.

Rule No. 3: Knowledge and practice of the language

Language is how you make sense of the experiences you've had across the globe. However, it is always just in part, and therefore does not actually provide exact information. You'll find that you utilize it more often to conceal than to bring attention to anything. For example, you may discover that you have a difficult time striking a balance between the three concepts of independence, interdependence, and reliance. You have a habit of communicating what you want other people to know but not what you want to keep to yourself.

The stimulation of the words that you utter is the initial level of communication on the semantic spectrum. The second level of meaning is your own interpretation of the world through the lens of your own experiences. The third component is the unique way in which you communicate that experience via the use of words. To put it another way, language is only a reflection of the things you've been through.

Welcoming you to the exciting realm of influence and persuasion! The idea of reciprocity will serve as the foundation for the rest of the principles that you will study. To reply to a gesture or action with a similar one of your own is what is meant by the word "reciprocate." Because this is a characteristic that is shared by the vast majority of people, we may utilize it to our advantage in order to persuade and influence other people.

When you want someone to do something for you, you should take the initiative and do something for that person first. This is a pretty straightforward way to apply the idea. When you go above and above for another person by taking the initiative to do something for them, that person develops a strong desire to return the favor in any manner you would want them to do it for you.

During one of my travels, I was able to make this observation. My journey from London to Paris was arranged via a travel agency, and I was looking forward to seeing the city of love. Following the completion of the booking process, the travel agent handed me a few vouchers. One of the coupons offered a chance to visit a perfume store and get a free bottle of fragrance if the customer redeemed it before the expiration date. I just could not stop myself from walking inside the perfume store and smelling several of the products at least once. When I went to the perfume store, rather of giving me a full-sized bottle of perfume, they provided me with little swabs of each of their wares to try. There were further customers in the store who were interested in taking advantage of the same deal, and all of them were offered the same thing. After I struck up a conversation with the sales representative there and established a connection with him, he provided me with a greater number of free samples than he had provided to any of the other customers. After seeing the kind deed that he had performed for me, I couldn't help but feel an overwhelming need to return the favor in some way. As a result of this, I found myself purchasing fragrances from his store. Simply due to the fact that the salesperson had helped me out so much, I felt the need to return the favor to him. I have no doubt that you, too, have been through something similar at some point in your life.

When working on this easy rule, there are a few things that you need to keep in mind in order to avoid making any mistakes. You are aware that you need to take the initial step, so as you are doing so, think about what you can do to help the other person. You can't simply do anything at random; you have to think of something that they would value if you did it for them. Only then would they feel the want to give something back in response to the gesture or act that you performed for them. Simple acts, such as providing a free sample, helpful advice, a small token of love in the form of a gift, inviting them over for a meal with you, or clearing a bill for them, or doing something for them that they were unable to do, are enough to arouse their desire to pay you back or do something for you in return of what you have done for them in response to the favors you have done for them.

Therefore, if you want other people to do anything for you, you need to show them that you care about them by helping them out first. This is a rule that you should never forget.

Both NLP And Hypnosis Are Quite Useful.

After looking at how you may use NLP in your everyday life, we will now examine how you can use it to influence the behaviour of other people.

People have the ability to persuade others to pay attention to what they have to say. Although it may seem to be a challenge to do, there is a good chance that it can be done.

You will need to be knowledgeable about the process, and you will undoubtedly have the ability to persuade people to pay attention to what you have to say and carry out your instructions.

In this chapter, we are going to have a look at some of the things that you may do to successfully influence other people and hypnotise them into doing what you say they should do.

To approach

Your initial step should be to initiate contact with the individual whose opinion you want to shape. The individual ought to be someone who you believe will unquestionably pay attention to what you have to say and carry out your instructions. The most effective strategy is to attempt to influence someone who has already been persuaded by you and is stunned by your charisma. This is the finest situation to put yourself in. You will almost certainly have someone of this sort working with you or within your group of friends. When you have determined who it will be, you should approach that person in the appropriate manner. Get their attention by calling them over to you, then stand with your back to them. You should be as charming as you possibly can and seem as presentable as you possibly can.

Trance (n.)

The next step is to make statements that will lead the other person to get completely absorbed in what you have to say. You need to choose your words with care and make sure that they are completely immersed in what you are saying. It is necessary for you to work towards having them read your lips. Avoid jumping right into the meat of the discussion. Before you give them the instructions, have something to discuss with them.

Talk it out.

Next, you will need to convey the instruction to them in a way that ensures they fully get it. You need to avoid making things too complicated and go straight to the point. For instance, if you want them to do something within a certain amount of time, you should make it very plain to them what it is that you want from them. You should also let them know that you are pinning a great deal of your hope on them, as this will instill a feeling of responsibility in them on your part. You need to make sure that they have properly grasped what you have informed them by having them repeat what you have spoken to them.

Tonality and pitch

When you are attempting to persuade someone, you need to be aware of the appropriate volume and cadence to utilise in your voice. If you want people to become excited about what you have to say, then you should talk in a very high tone. Additionally, you should speak in a low tone if you are attempting to demonstrate responsibility for anything. To ensure that your idea is understood in the clearest possible way, you must also speak in the appropriate manner.

Snap

The next step is to quickly snap your finger in order to bring them out of their trance. It can seem a little too academic, but you might have to do that in order to assist the individual in returning to their usual state of mind. Additionally, it will convey to them to go immediately to the duty that you have assigned to them. You may also do something more subtle to disturb their focus, such as brushing your shoulder or making some other gesture of the kind.

Iterate once more.

When you have found the perfect person to influence, it is imperative that you maintain a relationship with them. It is only at that point that you will be able to improve at it. Performing your activities repeatedly will not only help you build confidence but will also prepare you to go on to another individual who you can influence.

Where Does It Fall Within The Umbrella Of Nlp?

When it comes to neuro-linguistic programming, your mindset, including your attitude and viewpoint, is just as crucial as your imagination. What kind of person are you—optimistic, pessimistic, or realistic? Your perspective on the world will play a role in determining how well you are able to employ NLP. It is essential that you have the ability to differentiate between pessimists and optimists. Realists and pragmatics are two labels that may be applied to individuals who fall somewhere in the middle.

A constructive and upbeat perspective on one's life is the source of optimism. People that are optimistic see every circumstance in a positive light and are able to find the silver lining in every cloud. They also think that humans are naturally good and that the majority of people are content with their life. An other trait that distinguishes optimists from pessimists is their capacity to inspire confidence in others even under trying circumstances. It is not difficult to single out an optimist among a group of people. Their upbeat attitude might at times make it challenging for others to feel the same level of passion that they do. As is the case with other mental states, having an optimistic outlook may infect others around you. Spending time with a person who has a positive outlook on life may sometimes be beneficial in terms of lifting one's mood.

On the other hand, this does not mean that optimists are immune to being foolish. Even the most steadfast optimists are susceptible to having terrible days and experiencing negative feelings. It is also okay for them to have friends who are folks they don't trust or really like. The difference between pessimists and optimists is that optimists are firmly convinced that there is a bright side to every cloudy situation. People that are optimistic tend to be quite persistent. They are so certain that they will be successful in finding an answer or completing a job that they do not know how to give up on themselves.

Pessimism, on the other hand, is an unfavourable view. Pessimists are those who anticipate that unpleasant things will occur. Even though pessimism might be a difficult way to live, there are a lot of different reasons why it may present itself. People who have had a rough life may be more likely to have pessimistic views. People are inherently pessimists, therefore it's possible that their pessimism stems from the belief that they won't be let down if they anticipate the worst-case scenario. It's not that they have a preference for seeing things in a negative light. Anxiety and sadness are two examples of mental health conditions that might contribute to pessimism. A vicious cycle of pessimism and negativity that is brought on by mental illness may be difficult to stop. If you believe that your mental disease is the source of your pessimism, do not be afraid to seek the right counselling and therapy for your condition.

Both optimism and pessimism have the potential to infect others. Modelling may also be done via the process of mirroring. Mirroring and modelling will be examined in further depth in the next section. However, everyone in the room is able to sense the effect that one individual has on the overall atmosphere of the space. It is possible to convey to others what we are feeling and thinking via means other than words. It's possible that the way someone carries themselves and their entire vibe might have a larger influence on us than the words that are said directly to us.

Some individuals have a perspective on life that is agnostic. These individuals are either pragmatists or realists, depending on their outlook. Realists examine each circumstance in its whole and make judgements about it based on the merits of the scenario. Realists are pragmatic in their approach to problem-solving and hold the belief that there is a solution to every issue. They don't let their positive or negative attitudes influence their capacity to discover a solution to the problem.

Realists do not exist in an emotional void in their daily lives. They are also neither typically pessimists or optimists in their outlook on life. They are not affected by either positive or negative thoughts because they don't allow them. Realists analyse every facet of a predicament before deciding what the most effective next step should be. They are also aware of the fact that the "worst case scenario" is not always the greatest option.

After going through the many ways in which individuals may be categorised as thinkers, it is my goal that you will be able to recognise yourself in the aforementioned descriptors. Your next step will be to investigate when and how other individuals have their most creative thoughts.

What Kinds Of Effects Does Your Body Language Have On Your Mind?

The activities of the hands and arms, as well as the posture and actions of the body, as well as facial clues and eye motions, are all components of body language, which is an effective form of non-verbal communication. It conveys to people precisely what we are thinking, even when they do not fully grasp what we are saying.

We do a lot of this talking unknowingly, and in the same way, many individuals pick up on our non-verbal information without even being aware that they are doing it. The vast majority of us have no idea that our non-verbal cues are having an impact on others. There are hundreds of these teeny-tiny idioms, and people are reading them, even if they merely unconsciously interpret the allusions.

Signs of Manipulation Based on Body Language

Tricksters rely on a variety of strategies, one of which is deceptive body language, to obtain what they want. We came to the conclusion that individuals may engage in such motions as an emotional response to the stressful events that occur in their lives. On the other hand, if the individual isn't in a stressful setting and isn't exhibiting any other signs of worry, then this particular behaviour may point to some kind of manipulation. In point of fact, manipulators will utilise this old method of pacifying to acquire support from you, either consciously or unconsciously, in order to manage your actions.

Rubbing of the Neck and Hands

It might seem that con artists are rubbing their hands together in order to acquire what they desire. You might even see a clichéd cartoon villain laughing hysterically while rubbing their fingers together. Even Disney is aware that this behaviour is a hint that self-serving scheming is taking place. The manipulator may pretend to be anxious or melancholy in order to coerce you into agreeing to their terms by massaging their neck, which may indicate the same thing. And by caressing their neck, not only do they feel some regret for abusing you, but they are also neutralising the humiliation they feel for doing so. However, they are using you for their own benefit.

Picking at the Chin

When a con artist scratches their chin, they are attempting to give the impression that they are untrustworthy or hesitant. It is possible to convince someone to quit up and say, "It's okay," but doing so is not always easy. I am capable of doing it." If a person is entirely capable of the things you are thinking about doing while simultaneously scratching their chin, you may be certain that they are trying to deceive you into doing anything for them.

Touching and/or Stroking the Arm

It's possible that the person trying to influence you is trying to manipulate themselves when they touch or itch their arms. But of course, there are a variety of reasons why a person can scratch their arms; it might just be that they have been bitten by a bug! If, on the other hand, you have reason to believe that someone is trying to manipulate you but you see that they are scratching or rubbing their arms while they are talking to you, you might interpret this behaviour as an indication that they are trying to exert control over you.

Tap, tap, tap on the foot

The movements that manipulators make with their body are always the same. For example, they could stomp their foot or do anything else repetitive like tap their pen. This might be a sign of impatience or annoyance on their part, which they may exploit to try to persuade you to give in to what they want or act as they want you to. When individuals are tapping their feet, you are lot more likely to make a snap decision that may not be in their best interests and is much more likely to be impulsive.

How the Process of Body Language Operates

The activities of the hands and arms, as well as the posture and actions of the body, as well as facial clues and eye motions, are all components of body language, which is an effective form of non-verbal communication. It conveys to people precisely what we are thinking, even when they do not fully grasp what we are saying.

We do a lot of this talking unknowingly, and in the same way, many individuals pick up on our non-verbal information without even being aware that they are doing it. The vast majority of us have no idea that our non-verbal cues are having an impact on others. There are hundreds of these teeny-tiny idioms, and people are reading them, even if they merely unconsciously interpret the allusions.

Signs of Manipulation Based on Body Language

Tricksters rely on a variety of strategies, one of which is deceptive body language, to obtain what they want. We came to the conclusion that individuals may engage in such motions as an emotional response to the stressful events that occur in their lives. On the other hand, if the individual isn't in a stressful setting and isn't exhibiting any other signs of worry, then this particular behaviour may point to some kind of manipulation. In point of fact, manipulators will utilise this old method of pacifying to acquire support from you, either consciously or unconsciously, in order to manage your actions.

Rubbing of the Neck and Hands

It might seem that con artists are rubbing their hands together in order to acquire what they desire. You might even see a clichéd cartoon villain laughing hysterically while rubbing their fingers together. Even Disney is aware that this behaviour is a hint that self-serving scheming is taking place. The manipulator may pretend to be anxious or melancholy in order to coerce you into agreeing to their terms by massaging their neck, which may indicate the same thing. And by caressing their neck, not only do they feel some regret for abusing you, but they are also neutralising the humiliation they feel for doing so. However, they are using you for their own benefit.

Picking at the Chin

When a con artist scratches their chin, they are attempting to give the impression that they are untrustworthy or hesitant. It is possible to convince someone to quit up and say, "It's okay," but doing so is not always easy. I am capable of doing it." If a person is entirely capable of the things you are thinking about doing while simultaneously scratching their chin, you may be certain that they are trying to deceive you into doing anything for them.

Touching and/or Stroking the Arm

It's possible that the person trying to influence you is trying to manipulate themselves when they touch or itch their arms. But of course, there are a variety of reasons why a person can scratch their arms; it might just be that they have been bitten by a bug! If, on the other hand, you have reason to believe that someone is trying to manipulate you but you see that they are scratching or rubbing their arms while they are talking to you, you might interpret this behaviour as an indication that they are trying to exert control over you.

Tap, tap, tap on the foot

The movements that manipulators make with their body are always the same. For example, they could stomp their foot or do anything else repetitive like tap their pen. This might be a sign of impatience or annoyance on their part, which they may exploit to try to persuade you to give in to what they want or act as they want you to. When individuals are tapping their feet, you are lot more likely to make a snap decision that may not be in their best interests and is much more likely to be impulsive.

Hypnosis

Hypnosis refers to a state of consciousness that people may enter, in which they are no longer able to control the acts that they are doing. This is something that is often done in therapeutic settings in order to assist folks in finding the inner calm they need in order to tackle the most profound and insidious traumas they have experienced. Hypnosis also provides a method for convincing and influencing the opinions of other people.

Hypnosis and mind control may seem to be the same thing to some people since both entail exercising power or influence over another person. On the other hand, there are several striking differences between the two. In order for you to recognise the differences, it is vital that you become more familiar with the factors that determine them.

The state of hypnosis is one that has been intentionally created and is characterised by the individual's responsiveness to the hypnotist's questions and suggestions. The method may be carried out on a single person or on a group of individuals in order to accomplish a certain goal. When done for therapeutic reasons, this technique is referred to as hypnosis, and the procedure itself is known as hypnotherapy. In any event, the term "organised hypnosis" is often used to refer to the situation in which it is used as a method of diverting the attention of a large group of individuals.

Controlling one's personality, on the other hand, is the approach to make use of a few tricks in order to generate the perfect reaction you need from other people. You will be able to get either complete or partial command over what is occurring in the mind of another person by using the secret.

When used in the context of introspection, it has the potential to assist you in concentrating on the topic of your investigation.

When you take part in this kind of introspection, you give yourself the opportunity to work through your emotions and thoughts. As a general rule, amazing individuals who have achieved extraordinary success in life are able to have optimal mastery of their psyches by regularly reflecting on their experiences.

After going through the fundamental definitions of hypnosis and mind control, it should be easy to point out the differences between the two. The primary difference between the two that you will notice is that hypnosis can only be performed on other people. It is quite unlikely that there is any technique that may be used in order to hypnotise oneself. In order to successfully induce hypnosis, you will need the assistance of a subliminal expert.

However, personality control reflection may just as effectively be used on oneself as it can be used on other people.

You are free to engage in this kind of reflection whenever you see fit. There is no set time for it. Finding a quiet place, sitting down, and putting some thought into it is all that is required of you. Using mind control techniques, you can get other people to agree with you on certain points of contention.

When it comes to the method in which hypnosis is related with mind control, there is still another contrast that may be recognised. If the process of hypnosis was carried out with the appropriate attitude in mind, a trance expert may be able to assist you in breaking free from undesirable behaviours such as anxiety, smoking, or overeating.

Sometimes, the hypnosis professional may use a few techniques in the form of reflection to get people to feel comfortable recording the response they require at a certain moment in time. It is a very remote possibility that you will be able to spellbind someone by using mind control traps. Its primary function is to serve strategic goals.

It should come as no surprise that hypnosis and mind control are polar opposites of one another. Both of these things are not the same, despite the fact that some of the components that are used in one may also be used in the other. Everything depends on how well you are able to take into account the fundamental requirements that are involved.

The two primary aspects that make up hypnosis are known as acceptance and propositions. The primary suggestion that is sent throughout the hypnosis treatment is one of trancelike acceptance; however, the specifics of what this acceptance should include are up for debate.

It is usual practise to provide proposals to members in the form of recommendations, which elicit reflexive responses from those individuals since they do not believe they have a significant amount of or any influence over the condition. Additionally, some persons are more vulnerable to hypnosis than others, and researchers have observed that such individuals are more likely to have a diminished sense of authority when they are under the influence of hypnosis.

It has been suggested that susceptibility to hypnosis may be defined as the ability to experience postulated adjustments in one's physiology, sensations, sentiments, reflections, or behaviours. Neuroimaging techniques have shown that some people have increased levels of activity in the prefrontal cortex, primary cingulate cortex, and parietal regions of the mind during different stages of hypnosis.

These are areas of the brain that are linked to a wide variety of sophisticated mental capabilities, such as memory and observation, moods and the ability to pick up new tasks. However, the specific components of the brain that are involved in hypnosis are not completely understood at this time. The neuropsychological profile of this technique is, however, beginning to be sorted out by researchers.

How would one determine whether or not another person has been hypnotised? The individual is in a hypnotic trance, as shown by the many alterations that have occurred. These deep daze markers are a series of very thorough observations that one may make about the topic, and NLP refers to them as "profound daze markers." Practise and concentration are required in order to recognise such signs. In addition, the presence of just several of these indicators is sufficient to conclude that a patient is in a hypnotic state.

The Influence On Individuals

The goal of being a persuasive person, as well as the primary purpose of persuasion, is to achieve a desired result in exchange for one's efforts. When there is nothing to be gained in exchange for one's efforts to practice the art of persuasion, there is no use in doing so. To convince someone to act in a certain way is to employ the art of persuasion. As a consequence, attaining some kind of benefit or reaching some kind of conclusion is wanted.

It is necessary to have a well defined desired objective in order to know what the consequence of the endeavor to persuade is supposed to be. The one who is doing the convincing is looking for something concrete, something that can be defined. But what are they looking for? In any case, it is entirely up to them to decide, which often takes place before they engage in any kind of persuasion, which is precisely what they intend to do by the time the discussion is through with you.

In this sense, specifying intended outcomes refers to the process described above. Before beginning any form of persuasion strategy, it is necessary to define what it is that is being pursued; this ensures that the individual engaging in the persuasion is aware of the intended result.

For example, the employees of one office come to the conclusion that they need to conduct a conference in order to choose a new site for their company's office. This is due to the fact that the current office is seen as being too congested and tiny, while the company as a whole is experiencing expansion and thus need more space in order to continue its expansion. Therefore, there will be a meeting at the office during which a decision on the new site will be made. The first thing you need to do in order to define the desired result is to get familiar with the suggested outcome. In this instance, it refers to the place where the new office will be situated.

Therefore, the meeting will take place at the specified time and location that has been agreed upon. I take it you're done here? Not true! The conference will not be productive, and the result that was sought will most likely not be achieved, if there is not some kind of order and structure in place. The meeting is very important to achieving the result that was sought. In the absence of any kind of predetermined agenda, the meeting will amount to nothing more than a gathering of individuals in an office who have been gathered together for the purpose of conversing.

Therefore, it is vital to organize the meeting and come up with a game plan for how the discussion will go at this point. Because this is a meeting that incorporates the whole office personnel, it is possible that there will be no need to pick who to invite because everyone will be present. Consequently, the next thing that needs to be done is to prepare an agenda for the meeting; would there be time for questions? Will particular individuals be asked to participate and provide specific ideas for the new site if they are requested to do so? What criteria will be used to make the final selection? Before the start of the meeting, decisions need to be made about each of these aspects.

Make sure that you bring up the target result right at the beginning of the meeting. Make sure that everyone is aware of the topic that they are about to discuss. It is essential that all parties involved be aware of and comprehend the intended goal. Make sure to schedule a certain amount of time for both the conversation and the decision-making process. The next step is to repeat the aim when the conference draws closer to the conclusion of the allotted amount of time and to decide if a decision can be reached or whether further research is required.

An outcome is nothing more than a conclusion that can be seen and evaluated after it has been reached. It is the result that the activity has brought about. The result is the conclusion that comes about as a consequence of convincing someone to do something. Before settling on the desired result itself, there are first four things that have to be settled upon. This is true regardless of the end that is wanted. These are the four items to consider: is there a desire for anything in particular? Is it necessary to hold on to something that has already been acquired? Who should be linked, and how should that be done? Which abilities must be had in order to accomplish what must be done?

It is essential to make these choices since the underlying goals will undoubtedly have an impact on the path that must be taken in order to achieve the desired result. It's kind of like a football game where there's a defensive team and an offensive squad competing against one other. One group takes on the role of attacking the other team, while another group is responsible for defending themselves from assaults from the other team. Every group will have its own distinct order of priorities and system of operating processes. Their end goals will be quite different from one another in almost every way. Every group will have to determine if they wish to gain new knowledge, protect existing knowledge, or learn something new. The strategy will be devised based on the objective.

It has been determined what kind of modification is required, and that change will be implemented. The first step on the road to success is deciding what you want to accomplish. The target destination is the point where this voyage concludes. It is essential to have an understanding that these are two distinct entities that collaborate in order to attain the desired outcome.

A destination may be thought of as a goal. An outcome is a definite result that can be seen and evaluated in some way. Although determining the aim is necessary in order to achieve the result, the two are inherently distinct processes that need to be handled independently.

Reasons are always the driving force behind goals. Something that is believed to be required for pleasure, riches, or health, or just because it is really wanted, is simply absent from the situation. No matter what the cause may be, it is that reason in particular that propels forward movement toward the conclusion that is wanted. To be able to advance, to make headway toward the objective, it is necessary for you to have both the objective and the concept of reaching it ingrained deeply in your mind. If one does not maintain a consistent concentration on the target, there is no chance that the target will ever be accomplished.

Imagine having to go to the same job every day for the next fifteen years, no matter how much you advance in your career. Imagine that this is a job that required college coursework, and you picked it because of that requirement. Over the course of the previous fifteen years, it has been enjoyable and lucrative to do the exact same work each and every day. There have been a number of promotions, the most recent of which included a private secretary as well as a gorgeous huge office space. Every Monday at this enormous new office, the team that directly reports to you now consists of many additional employees, some of whom have not been working here nearly as long as others have been.

Deception

It's been done by everyone. Young youngsters are unable to determine who was responsible for making the mess or breaking the light. The cheque has been sent out to you. In the next five minutes, we will be ready. Yes, the outfit complements your figure quite well. The white lie, if you will. It is ingrained in the essence of humans. Let's take a look at the reasons behind why we tell falsehoods before we go on to discussing how we might utilize them.

Lies!

Why is it that people are biologically programmed to lie? Where does the natural inclination to lie originate from? Is it psychological, biological, or a combination of the two? Both is the correct response! The 'tend and defend' reaction is the psychological mechanism that causes humans to tell lies. This indicates that falsehoods are employed to respond to needs or to guard against the danger, and there is a link between lying and the production of the brain chemical oxytocin, which is one of our inherent 'feel good' hormones. When our levels of oxytocin are high, we have a greater propensity to tell lies in order to prevent ourselves from losing that sense of a natural high.

There are a number of well-documented explanations for why people lie; these explanations may be categorized as either defend or trend. The following are some of them:

1- Defend oneself: these are lies made to avoid punishment or backlash for action or perceived action; 2- Defend others: these are lies made to avoid others being punished or attacked for their actions or perceived actions; 3- Tend to oneself: these are lies told to gain control of a situation or a person, lies told to avoid embarrassment or awkward social situations, or lies told to gain personal desires or win admiration; and 4- Tend to others: lies told to pry information out of others or

It is not necessary for a lie to be something so catastrophic in order for it to be problematic for a person's ability to keep their tale straight when it is too large. It is said that the finest falsehoods have some element of truth, and it would seem that this is the case. When lies are exposed, they often have severe repercussions, so if you plan on engaging in deception, you should ensure that you are mentally and emotionally ready to cope with any backlash that may occur.

The consequences of Pinocchio's falsehoods revealed themselves physically in the development of a larger nose!

Applications of NLP in the business world

Consultants who are skilled in NLP may also provide assistance to company owners and managers in the form of another kind of coaching. Problems with creativity may sometimes be helped by using methods like the Disney Strategy. When there is a problem with restricting assumptions about the future of a company, one solution is to apply the timeline example that was just described.

Enhancing company communication may also be accomplished via the use of a vast array of methods, some of which include the leadership process and the sales process. If you have a working knowledge of NLP theory, it will be much simpler for you to comprehend the ways in which your employers, suppliers, and consumers or clients communicate and think. After running your verbal and written communication through their own filters, every single one of them will comprehend what you are saying and writing. You will be able to speak with them in a language that they are more at ease with if you learn to know their values, beliefs, and meta-programs first. This will allow you to have a meaningful conversation with them.

This is simply one more illustration of how to utilize rapport effectively in challenging circumstances. The abilities of rapport that I covered in the previous section on Developing Instant Rapport most surely apply to this situation as well, of course. When you understand the significance of anchoring states, you'll also be able to appreciate the significance of any and every communication about the marketing of ideas, goods, and services. As a result, an experienced NLP Practitioner, whether they work as a consultant, a trainer, or the management or owner of the business, will have the ability to modify anchors or meta-programs so that their clients may achieve greater levels of success.

8. Use a person's history to have an impact on their future.

Do you have any idea how much the things you learnt when you were younger have influenced the person you are today? Have you observed that the manner in which a person's parents and teachers shaped their upbringing has an effect on the person's present capabilities, as well as their anxieties and limitations? The outcome that may be produced in this day and age is virtually mathematical. We may even apply an equation: impact = our parents' education times the amount of education we've received.

Do you want some real-world illustrations to back up this assertion? There is nothing better than the numerological challenges to show us the influence—positive or negative—of the way we were taught, and there is nothing greater than the problems themselves. The numbers in this position symbolize the anxieties that had to be confronted and triumphed over with the assistance of our parents. It exemplifies the types of mentalities and actions that we shudder at the prospect of acquiring and partaking in. As a result, the manner in which our parents and teachers responded to similar challenges when we were younger may reflect whether or not we perceive these challenges with dread or as an opportunity for differentiation in our conduct now.

Therefore, it is beneficial to do this investigation into the past in order to have an understanding of the potential consequences that the education you got has on your current situation.

The origin of a phobia

Your fear of whatever it is that you want to get rid of will be eliminated as a result of this.

And this one is almost like an inverted version of the previous method.

Needles fall under my usage.

I had a severe phobia of needles for a good portion of my life.

Because to this method, I was able to overcome my phobia of needles.

The first thing that comes to me is viewing a video of myself getting pricked by needles.

After that, I see someone poking a needle into my arm and feeling the needle break the skin on my arm.

After that, I was able to see the physician and have my blood drawn for testing.

(Once again, you may either have someone read this to you or go through each step in order.)

We hope you like this updated, more sanitary version.

How severe is your fear when ranked on a scale from one to ten?

Imagine you're in the theater, and you're about to attend a movie.

It is a video of you engaging in your fear, and in the movie, you remain calm and collected throughout the experience.

You are now seated in a movie theater, seeing a film of yourself engaging in the activity that gives you the most anxiety.

And in this movie, you remain calm and collected even while you face your worst fears front on.

Let the video play for a minute while you see yourself engaging in the behavior that you want to avoid.

You are now truly engaging in the behavior that you dread.

What would you see, what would you hear, and how would it feel on your skin if you did this?

While you are facing your greatest fear, you take a few slow, deep breaths.

Have a good laugh at yourself for being so afraid to carry out this task.

Imagine that it is one month from now, and that you have finally worked up the courage to face your phobia.

On a scale from one to ten, how mild is the phobia at the moment?

Perform this approach once again, but this time in a completely new environment.

Methods To Gain Control Over Yourself, And Consequently, Your Life

There are two distinct ways that one might go through life.

One takes on the role of a victim, experiencing feelings of resentment and frustration in response to the challenges presented by life, and attempting to influence the behavior of others around them in order to improve their quality of life.

The second is similar to a wizard in that they take all that life throws at you and use it to enhance themselves. This makes them stronger and more adaptable, which in turn makes life easier and more enjoyable.

Have you ever considered switching up your strategy in the event that you've been squandering your efforts by attempting to influence the individuals in your immediate environment or by adjusting your behavior to accommodate the circumstances of your life?

How about instead of utilizing one's passion to better oneself, one uses it to make other people's experiences and challenging circumstances easier?

However, the same quantity of energy is involved. A really distinct and unexpected result.

The operation is as follows:

1. Don't let yourself get caught up in the blame game.

This is a significant piece of evidence that points to you as a possible criminal. If you blame other people of having caused your experience, you are giving up your control and making your experience dependent on the actions of other people. Which presupposes that you use all of your available resources in an effort to persuade other individuals to alter the way in which they are behaving so that you might have a different experience.

In my most recent committed relationship, I have spent much too much time acting the part of the victim. Before we began hanging out together, my ex-partner had already begun weaning herself off of cannabis. When that occurred, he was on the verge of leaving the company.

After three and a half years, I was still holding out hope that he would leave so that I wouldn't have to go out with an alcoholic and deal with all that comes along with it. I eventually came to the realization that the main reason I was still hanging around with an alcoholic was not because he was unable to go, but rather because I was unable to stop myself from doing so. This is the end of him. As a result, I did that. sever ties with the other person. The issue has been addressed and resolved.

NLP Techniques That Have Undergone Behavioral Alterations

This chapter focuses on the most effective NLP approaches for bringing about beneficial behavioral changes, which are discussed throughout the rest of the book. There are five of them that I will be describing in this article, and they are as follows:

Dissociation, Reframing of the Content, and Anchoring Yourself in the World

Creating a Sense of Compatibility

Dissociation Resulting From Shifting Beliefs

This is a frequent strategy used in neuro-linguistic programming (NLP) to stop people from having knee-jerk responses, which may lead them to behave in a way that they would later come to regret. The process of dissociation is useful in neutralizing unpleasant sentiments and emotions in any given scenario, whether it's because a buddy is running late to pick you up for a party or because there are problems at work. The following is a list of the measures that you may take to detach yourself from unfavorable emotions:

1. To begin, you should determine the sensation that you are now experiencing. Is it anger or hate or discomfort or distaste of the circumstance or something else entirely?

2. At this point, put yourself in the position of the observer and try to perceive things from their point of view.

3. After that, bring your attention back to yourself and keep feeling the emotion. Keep in mind that you should not answer. It would be interesting to see

this movie from both your perspective and that of an observer.

4. At this point, go forward in the movie so that it is playing more quickly in your head. As you play this movie in your head, give it a humorous music to accompany the scenes you're seeing in your head.

5. When you bring yourself back to the present now and focus on the activity that is taking place, you will discover that the unfavorable feelings have simply evaporated into thin air.

Reframing of the Content

This is an excellent strategy to use when you are in a predicament in which you feel like you have no control. You have the ability to modify the meaning of your experience simply by reframing the events that took place throughout it. For instance, if the termination of a toxic relationship was very difficult for you, this might be a really traumatic experience. Now, all you need to do is make a conscious effort to alter the nature of this experience and look at it from the point of view of liberation.

Examine the event through the lens of how much you were able to pick up from it. Your experience may be reframed in such a manner that it shifts the attention away from the bad emotions you are experiencing. This adjustment will assist you in managing the challenges that have surfaced as a result of such bad events. It is true that while dealing with a lot of stress, it may be quite difficult to feel and see anything other than dread and terror. However, you need to keep in mind that these worries will only make the situation more difficult, and diverting your attention away from them can help you deal with the stressful conditions more effectively.

Techniques From The Field Of Neuro-Linguistic Programming That May Be Used To Create Anchors

In this section, we will discuss how to construct grapples with a variety of different approaches. A grapple might be seen of as a switch that turns on a passionate current inside you. The sensations produced by grappling may range from exhilarating to excruciating. The affiliation principle is the guiding principle. If we associate a certain stimulus with a particular emotion, we can almost guarantee that we will experience that emotion every time the trigger is activated.

You may have heard of an exceptionally well-known experiment that Ivan Pavlov conducted on the subject of the passionate training of mutts. In the event that you are unaware of it, I suggest that you look up the investigation on Google after typing the phrase into the search engine and reading about it. This study demonstrated that it was possible to produce a predetermined excited response with a trigger or stay (right now ringing chime), provided that the subject (the dog) was pre-adapted to that reaction.

In terms of individuals, the counterpart is the chief. We each have our own unique grappling mechanisms built within us. The problem is that the vast majority of us are either unaware that these stumbling blocks exist or that they have an effect on who we are as individuals. There is a diverse variety of possible formats in which grapples may be realized. They may be staying reliant on the immediate environment, on solidity, on touch, or on any other of the faculties.

It is more convenient to provide a specific example. Let's say that 10 years ago, you attended to a memorial ceremony for an aunt of yours who you loved without a shadow of a doubt, and let's also say that the occasion was quite emotional for you. They burned incense as part of the memorial service, which was an important part of the ceremony. It was obvious that you were in the midst of a very emotional argument. You inhaled deeply, taking in the distinctive aroma of the incense.

After 10 years have passed, you come upon a store on your way to work. You are aware that there is something specific about the store that makes you feel terribly depressed, but you are unable to make sense of exactly what it is about the business that is causing you to feel this way. Taking everything into consideration, it is a beautiful day in the summer, and you are looking forward to your vacation.

In spite of the fact that you aren't consciously aware of it, the store you're in is really burning an incense brand that was present during the funeral ceremony for your aunt. The scent that you are taking in is triggering an instinctive reaction that is reminding you of the sentiments that you had when attending the funeral ceremony for your auntie. After 10 years have passed, you realize that despite everything, you continue to have the same sentiments. The incense's aroma is the challenge, while the negative mental state you experienced as a consequence of the situation is the outcome.

As can be seen, the struggle takes place on an intuitive level, and it is rooted in the belief that the way you are feeling right now is the direct result of your prior engagement in activities involving heightened states of desire. It's possible that the occasion in question was a happy one, like a wedding or another happy event of a similar kind. At this very moment, the thoughts and emotions that are brought to the forefront are reliable ones. Regardless of the circumstances, the norm is that there was a trigger, and as a result, an adjustment was made to the state of mind. This is the process that is used to create grapples, which is also the way in which they bring about true behavioral changes in people.

The Application of Neuro-Linguistic Programming to Produce a Life That Is Remarkably Calm, Productive, and Well-Balanced

I'll offer you the definition of Neuro-Linguistic Programming (also commonly referred to as NLP) in a more gradually justifiable form rather than providing you the specialized breakdown of what the lengthy phrase Neuro-Linguistic Programming (also commonly referred to as NLP) is. Neuro-Linguistic Programming, often known as NLP, is defined as "using the language of the brain or sensory system to reliably and effectively make your ideal outcomes throughout everyday life." NLP is an acronym that stands for Neuro-Linguistic Programming. Because it refers to a person's sensory system, the word "neuro" is often used in medical and scientific contexts. The term "semantic" is used because it refers to the language or other forms of non-verbal communication through which your sensory system obtains data. This is the reason why the term is used. In conclusion, the term "writing computer programs" is used because, regardless of whether we want to admit it or not, in all honesty, everything about us right now is the result of some kind of shaping that has happened either via our conscious awareness or unwittingly. This is the reason why the word "writing computer programs" is used.

As was previously shown, the majority of the time we are molded into something. It goes without saying that if we have good and enabling qualities and practices ingrained into our sensory system, then that is an incredible development. However, in reality, we as a whole have some negative or constraining moldings, such as anxieties and fears, ways of behaving or conceiving that in some way or another produces pain and damage ourselves or others, and ignorant obstacles that are keeping us from attaining our goals.

Assuming for the most part that we are the result of molding, it would obviously be beneficial to expose any restrictive molding that is now in place and replace it with something constructive if this is the case. Due to the fact that the strategies and procedures that are a part of Neuro-Linguistic Programming (also known as NLP) were expressly developed for this purpose, this is the point at which NLP becomes uncomfortable.

You, or rather a sensory system, are caused by Neuro-Linguistic Programming to dissociate themselves from the limiting instances that the program has coded and stored. To put it more simply, it helps shatter old, limiting instances that are no longer helping you well in any way.

As soon as that step is through, the next thing that NLP does is assistance by coordinating and molding into your sensory system the good examples that you need that will assist you as you continue to move forward. In the unlikely event that it hasn't already occurred to you, everything that is ingrained into your sensory system or mind is subject to some kind of computerization. Things like smoking, biting your fingernails, being startled by snakes, having a hypersensitivity to certain things, having a tendency to linger, and so on are completely adapted into your sensory system, and everything necessary for the example of conduct or dread and so forth to run is making sure conditions in your condition are met. Therefore, I have no doubt that you are aware that removing such limiting restrictions at this time would result in a significant amount of positive outcomes.

Methods For Influencing The Mind

Is it feasible for one person to exert influence on the thoughts and behaviours of another? This is a worry that a lot of people have; nobody wants other people to influence their thoughts without their permission, and nobody wants to see it happen. The idea and notion of manipulating the minds of other people is what gave rise to the phrase "mind control," which is often used in most conspiracy theories in which entities or organisations such as the government or extraterrestrials are accused of managing human minds. Controlling the mind of another person entails exerting an influence on that person's thinking, which may be rather powerful in some circumstances. On the other hand, there is no assurance that every single individual can be affected by the use of methods for mind control.

Controlling someone's mind is also referred to as thought reform, manipulation, mental control, brainwashing, coercive control, coercive persuasion, malicious use of group dynamics, and a number of other names. There is a lack of consensus on the precise meaning of the phrase due to the fact that it is used to designate so many different kinds of control. As a result, this disagreement allows for distortion and misunderstanding, particularly on the part of those individuals who are using mind control tactics for the purpose of furthering their own egotistical interests. Let's say, for the sake of our research, that we accept the premise that methods of mind control fall under the category of forms of influence and persuasion. The goal of any attempt at mind control is to get a person to act differently and believe different things than they now do.

There are others who believe that everything is the product of some kind of manipulation. If we refer to the whole process of mind control as manipulation, however, we run the risk of blurring essential differences. Manipulation is often used as a pejorative term to describe undesirable characteristics in individuals. It is more beneficial to conceive of influence as a continuum when evaluating mind control and the strategies that are used for it. At one end of the continuum is a collection of positive and ethical influences, and at the other end is a collection of negative and manipulative influences. Some methods of mind control are respectful of the individual, however other methods are damaging and have a tendency to rob a person of all of his or her individuality, capacity to think rationally or critically, and independence.

This unfavourable conclusion is exactly what we are trying to prevent. This is a typical location for the presence of self-serving manipulators and persuaders, as well as cults and sects. These individuals take advantage of other people by manipulating their thoughts via various mind control methods and by lying to them. They use the vulnerabilities and strengths of their victims in order to fulfil the requirements of their own self-centered desires. People in one-on-one cults are responsible for the majority of the tactics that are utilised for mind control. One on one cult is a term used to describe an intimate connection in which one person utilises his or her authority to exploit another person. This kind of interaction may be between a therapist and a client, a teacher and a student, a woman and her husband, a pastor and a worshipper, and so on. The fundamental cultic connections described above are scaled-down counterparts of bigger group cults; nevertheless, due to the fact that all of the focus and energy is concentrated on a single individual, they pose a greater risk.

How Should One Go About Using The Anchoring Technique?

It is recommended that before beginning this method, you choose a private spot where you won't be bothered by anybody else and make yourself comfortable there. Only then should you begin the procedure. As soon as it is finished, you may go on to the other steps of the anchoring method, which are as follows:

Choose an emotion that you want to have in some circumstance at some point in the near or far future. Your ideal state of mind may be represented by any emotion. Take, for instance, the states of being driven, calm, joyful, or energised.

Now, cast your mind into the far past and try to recollect the specific instance in which you felt exactly the same way in the past. Be careful to choose a powerful experience that showcases this specific sensation or emotion at its peak intensity. When you think about what happened, you will immediately start to feel like you did at that time all over again.

If you haven't been through something like to this before, I want you to visualise what it would be like to feel that way and then put yourself in a scenario that would cause you to feel the same way. If you can do that, then I'll consider it a success. When you are trying to establish your anchor, the circumstances surrounding the recollection are irrelevant. When you think back on those times, the sensation that you remember is the only thing that really counts.

Put your eyes out and try to recall that sensation in as much detail as possible; then transport yourself to the time and place where it occurred and recreate it with the maximum intensity. It seems as if your sensation is becoming stronger all the time.
Bring the hues of that picture in your mind's eye into better focus. Make the image more distinct and distinct.
Make sure that the noises of the occurrence can be heard more clearly.

Imagine that there is a screen in your head, and then transfer the pictures you're thinking about onto that screen.

Find a term that can best describe that sensation, and use that word. For example, excellent, wonderful, remarkable, or faultless.

Launch your one-of-a-kind anchor for this sensation at the precise moment when it is at its most potent and the degree of intensity is at its peak. Your anchor may consist of nothing more than a single motion, such as squeezing your left palm or pressing your index finger to your thumb, for example. Pick a hand gesture that best suits you and your needs.

Now, shake off the emotion you just had by diverting yourself or moving about and letting go of the frame of mind you've been in.

Anchoring must be done once more in this procedure.

Your intended sensation or emotion will get secured in your mind once you have completed the anchoring technique a few more times. You will be able to evoke the same feeling each and every time you do the gesture that you choose, which is the action that you carried out in step 3.

Try letting go of the anchor and seeing whether the sensation returns with the same level of intensity as it did while you were establishing it.

If the sensation is not as powerful and intense as you had hoped, continue the procedure of anchoring as many times as necessary until you are able to obtain the desired level of intensity.

The Function of Hypothesis

The following is a list of the roles that this theory fulfils:

The process of observation and experimentation is made easier by hypotheses.

It serves as the primary point of departure for the inquiry.

The verification of observations is helped along by hypotheses.

It points the inquiry in the appropriate direction, which is helpful.

How might hypotheses contribute to the overall success of the scientific method?

Hypotheses are used by researchers to help them form their thoughts and to guide them while they carry out studies. The following is a list of the stages that are included in the scientific method:

The emergence of a problem

Carry out some preliminary study.

Establishment of the Hypothesis

Conceive of an experiment.

Gathering of information

Evaluation of the Results

Experimentation summary

The consequences of the exchange

The Origins and Development of Hypnosis

The usage of hypnosis may be dated back to at least 500 BC, when it was used in what was known as the "Sleep Temple" in Greece. This temple was constructed with the express purpose of treating patients who suffered from mental health conditions. The priest will perform a rite that will cause them to "fall asleep," and after they are sleeping, the priest will recount the dream that the "patient" had in an effort to ward off the "evil" spirit. When we take a dispassionate look at the situation, we can see that this is a therapy that has been offered to us; however, there is no record to inform us how effective they are. The Austrian scientist Franz Anton Mesmer (1734–1815), who lived in the 18th century, had a significant impact on the present conception of the hypnotist. Mesmer is often credited with being the one who first introduced hypnotism to the notice of the general public. Because he referred to it at the time as "animal magnetism" rather than hypnotism, no one knew about it. Mesmer hypothesised that illness resulted from the magnetic field in our bodies being disrupted, coming into conflict with one another, or flowing in the incorrect direction. Following his observation of the magnetite (magnet) being handled by an almost unheard-of kind of street "magic" at the time, he came up with this fairly peculiar notion. Because the people who listened to Messmer had never seen anything like this before, they were in wonder when he demonstrated how his "magic wand" could attract, repel, and move iron ore.

An interesting incident revolves around a street artist who explained magnetism to the gathering and said that everyone had magnetic properties. After that, he began telling specific individuals that if he touched them with a magician's wand, it would alter the Magnetism in their bodies. This was after he had already done so. Someone in this situation is going to fall to the ground and start laughing, then someone else is going to fall to the ground and start crying, and so on. Mesmer was taken aback when any suggestion took place, and it is likely at that time that he came to the conclusion that if the magnetic field were to be oriented in the incorrect way, then people would get ill. Mesmer was adamant about putting this incredible medical occurrence to the test, and he rapidly learned that he could deliver evident miraculous cures for a variety of illnesses. In the 1780s, individuals were standing in line at the famed Paris Salon because Messmer (Messmer) had achieved remarkable success in the treatment of their condition. Because he was unable to treat everyone, he came up with some incredibly innovative treatments in order to assist all of the people who sought his assistance. One of them is to exert his magnetic influence on a tree in the backyard by making contact with the tree using one of his "magnet sticks." Many of the individuals who have sought his advice are unable to even see him. They have been given the instruction to stroke the magnetised tree, and regardless of the illness that they have, they will get well after doing so.

The second innovative approach that he devised requires nothing more than a pail of sand and the pulling of a few ropes from the bucket. To alleviate their problems, his patient has to do nothing more than sit around the barrel and grasp a rope. This is the power of suggestion in the Western world before the impact of science and education. Benjamin Franklin, a well-known physicist and diplomat from the United States, is generally credited for blowing the Mesmer bubble. In 1785, when he was about 80 years old, he was selected by the French government as one of the three committees to research Mesmer's powers precisely. Franklin was a popular and respected person in France at the time, and he was picked to serve on one of the committees because of his prominence in France at the time. Now, it seemed as if he understood the situation very fast, since he said, "If these people get better, then they will do it by their imagination." Although it is just a suggestion and not an imagination, neither he nor Mesmer himself realised how strong the suggestion was. Of course, this is simply a suggestion. Despite Franklin's rejection of his practise, which led to the method's notoriety, Messmer is still considered to be one of the most iconic individuals in the area of therapy. Even in modern times, people continue to use the word "Mesmerised," which often refers to a certain level of penetrating or immobilising influence.

Messmer was the one who thought of passing the hand around or near the body while doing the exercise. Many people continue to believe that this is one of the hypnotist's trade secrets, and that he did it by moving the subject inside the magnetic field that he envisioned. Hand. What exactly does it mean when someone says that Mesmer's animal magnetism is hypnosis? James Braid (1795-1860) was a Scottish ophthalmologist who lived during that time period. He experimented with this occurrence and came up with the term "Hypnosis" after the ancient Greek substance Hypnos, which was used to induce sleep. After seeing the beginning of hypnotism, he gave the practise the term hypnosis and then used it on a little girl to demonstrate its effectiveness. He was so amazed when she did not exhibit any symptoms of pain that he went on to undertake endless trials for himself and finally gave the procedure a new name that was incorrect. Later on, when Brad saw his error, he decided to rename it to "single consciousness," which means to focus on just one train of thought. Since it had nothing to do with sleeping, he felt this was a more appropriate term. The concept of induced sleep, which some believe may result in supernaturally thrilling experiences, is popular among the general population.

It seems as if the medium has reached the tr stage, at least to some level. They won't settle for uninteresting clinical titles as alternatives, thus hypnotism will be around for a very long time. Emile Coué, a Frenchman who lived from 1857 through 1926, did away with conventional procedures and began using automatic suggestion instead. The most well-known phrase he ever spoke was, "Every day is getting better and better." In addition to this, he is aware of the significance of the subjects who actively participate in the hypnosis process and was an early pioneer of practitioners. They have come to the conclusion that "there is no such thing. Clark Hull, a pioneer in the field of hypnotism, and Milton H. Erickson, a student in the field at the time were primarily responsible for the adoption of hypnotism in contemporary medicine. The 1920s and 1930s were the beginning of the research. Erickson is still widely regarded as the preeminent expert in clinical hypnosis and the preeminent practitioner of indirect hypnosis. He is able to induce "tr" in his subjects without ever so much as uttering the word "hypnosis." The Erickson technique and all of its many offshoots are widely regarded as the most efficient form of technology. Milton Erickson passed away in 1980, yet he was followed by many others.

How Can You Overcome Your Tendency To Procrastinate With The Help Of NLP Techniques?

Many NLP practitioners have confessed that one of the reasons they joined in our NLP certification programme was to acquire beneficial NLP strategies for overcoming procrastination. This is just one of the many benefits that can be gained by taking part in our NLP training.

You, too, presumably have been suffering from this debilitating disease and illness for a considerable amount of time, just like they have. You are aware of the repercussions that might arise as a result of your incapacity to break free from this destructive procrastination pattern, and you want to take action.

Now the question is, "Of the many NLP strategies, is there one that can effectively assist you in overcoming procrastination?"

There is one strategy that a significant number of our practitioners have reported having success with.

You will get acquainted with an effective strategy that may help you overcome procrastination and also goes one step further than that. This strategy will become available to you as soon as possible. Transform your tendency to put things off into a source of power!

In point of fact, many NLP practitioners utilise a strategy known as "chaining anchors" as a means of overcoming the effects of procrastination.

However, before we get into utilising NLP chaining anchors, let's take a look at the reasons why people put things off.

There are numerous potential reasons for putting things off till later. On the other hand, the primary reason for this is often a lack of motivation to do anything in their life. When we do not have the drive to accomplish a life objective, our natural tendency is to continually rest on our laurels. We have a tendency to hold ourselves back from doing the things that are required to obtain the result that we seek.

Therefore, if we find ourselves beginning to procrastinate, we have to force ourselves into a state of motivation.

Because the state of motivation is usually rather far away, professionals often need to construct a bridge or a chain of anchors in order to "transport" folks from their present position to the one that they have identified as being desirable.

When you feel as if it will take a lot of work to get yourself out of a "stuck" state (uncertainty, procrastination, perplexity, etc.), chaining anchors may be very helpful in getting you into a state of motivation so that you can get started.

Chaining anchors are a technique that may be used in NLP to help people overcome procrastination.

1. To get started with the process, you should begin by figuring out the phases in between procrastination and inspiration that you feel will help you make the shift from one to the other. It is very important to investigate the severity of these states (i.e., are they potent enough to go farther up the chain?).

2. How does it make you feel to put off taking action? What is it that you most often do while you are procrastinating your work? Continue the process with

some of your other prior encounters. Change the status of.

3. Establish a fixed point for each of the intermediate states. A broken state has to be carried out first, before anchoring on any subsequent state.

4. Maintain your concentration on the desired or completed level of motivation. It is important to get the most out of the usefulness of this positive anchor.

5. Work your way through the chain of anchors by releasing each one in turn as the situation becomes more likely to worsen and then fire the next anchor in the chain. To condition the chaining anchor, it is necessary to do this method numerous times. It is necessary for the anchor to have complete freedom of movement throughout the chain. Change the status of.